HOW DO WE KNOW
WHERE
PEOPLE
CAME FROM?

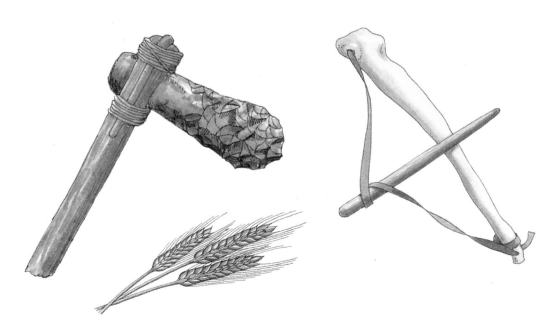

MIKE CORBISHLEY

RSVP
RAINTREE
STECK-VAUGHN
PUBLISHERS
The Steck-Vaughn Company

Austin, Texas

Published by Raintree Steck-Vaughn Publishers, an imprint of Steck-Vaughn Company

Commissioning Editor: Thomas Keegan
Designer: Hammond Hammond
Editors: Kate Scarborough and Maurice J. Sabean
Consultant: Jaymie L. Brauer, Collection Associate, Anthropology Department, American Museum of Natural History

Library of Congress Cataloging-in-Publication Data
Corbishley, Mike.
 Where people came from? / Mike Corbishley.
  p.   cm. — (How do we know)
 Includes index.
 ISBN 0–8114–3880–5
 1. Man, Prehistoric—Juvenile literature.   2. Civilization, Ancient—Juvenile literature.   [1. Man, Prehistoric.
 2. Civilization, Ancient.]   I. Title.   II. Series.
 GN744.C66   1995
 930.1—dc20   94–16651
                                                      CIP
                                                      AC

Printed and bound in Hong Kong
1 2 3 4 5 6 7 8 9 0 HK 99 98 97 96 95 94

Picture Acknowledgements
AKG, p. 25; Aerofilms, p. 34; Birmingham Public Libraries, p. 9t; The Bridgeman Art Library, p. 32; British Museum, p. 13tl; J. Allen Cash, p. 8; Colorific, p. 23t; Mike Corbishley, pp. 34, 39; Joanna Defreitas, p. 18; C.M. Dixon, p. 15t; English Heritage, pp. 7, 35bl and br; Werner Forman Archive, p. 9bl; Robert Harding Picture Library, pp. 14r, 23b; Michael Holford, pp. 12bl, 15b, 31cl and cr, 38c; NHPA, p. 30t; Scala, p. 30b; School of Biological Sciences, University of Manchester, p. 38b; Telegraph Colour Library, p. 16. All illustrations supplied by Simon Girling and Associates.

The words in boldface type are explained in the glossary.

Contents

Where People Came From?

How old is the Earth we live on? We think it was formed about 4.6 billion years ago. About 3.5 billion years ago, life on Earth began with little **organisms**, resembling bacteria. Then creatures such as worms and jellyfish developed in the oceans. It wasn't until about 400 million years ago that animals began living on land. Many species of animals lived and then became extinct. Among these were the dinosaurs, which lived on Earth for over 140 million years but died out suddenly about 65 million years ago. Human beings arrived much later.

Scientists use the term **evolution** to describe the way in which we think humans developed from other species of animals on Earth. Human beings are closely related to the great apes—animals such as gorillas. Both apes and humans seem to have shared the same ancestor millions of years ago. It is difficult for scientists to be absolutely sure because there is relatively very little evidence to go on. The scientists who study the development of the earliest peoples on Earth are called anthropologists.

We think that about 10 million years ago, the climate on Earth was gradually changing. In Africa grassland was replacing dense forests. The apes who lived there began to collect food from the grasslands. They may have started to walk upright because they no longer lived in trees and so did not need to hold on to the branches. These apes must have learned to work together as they collected their food and scavenged from dead animals. We call the first of the early humans *Australopithecus*, which means "southern ape."

THE DEVELOPMENT OF PEOPLE
Only the bones of the earliest people and their ancestors have been found. Sometimes the bones were fossilized, or turned to stone. Anthropologists and **archaeologists** (people who study the remains of people from the past) have very little evidence from these early peoples. The evidence is usually skeletons, or skeleton parts, and the tools they used. However, this evidence is enough to show us a kind of progression. The earliest skeletons show traces of similarity to later types. But the differences are striking. Evidence of the earliest peoples and their ancestors have been found in Africa.

Australopithecus
The *Australopithecus* species seems to have been a combination of ape and human. They walked upright and had teeth similar to ours today. We know they were living in Africa from at least 3.7 million years ago. Anthropologists have discovered at least four different types of *Australopithecines*.

Homo habilis
The most primitive member of our own genus is called *Homo habilis*. We know this species existed 2 to 1.5 million years ago in Africa. The first *Homo habilis* bones were found in Olduvai Gorge in Tanzania. *Homo habilis* was the first species to make tools.

FINDS AT LAETOLI

The oldest footprints in the world were found at a place now known as Laetoli in Tanzania, East Africa. They are 3.7 million years old. In 1976 archaeologists found the footprints of two members of the *Australopithecus* species. One set of prints was large, and the other was small, but we can't tell if they were made by males or females. They had walked over ground of soft volcanic ash. After they had gone, it must have rained, and the surface became rock hard. Their footprints were preserved. Other ashy deposits covered the footprints until they were rediscovered. From work carried out by archaeologists, we know that the area around the footprints was grassland with a few trees. There were a few lakes as well.

Homo ergaster
This species was living about 1.5 million years ago in Africa but had died out by about 300,000 years ago. *Homo ergaster* were the first humans to use fire and were good at making different kinds of tools.

Homo neanderthalensis
By 150,000 years ago, there was a new species of humans in the world. These people did not look quite the same as we do today. They had flatter heads and were stockier in build. They were an advanced people—they buried their dead and probably had some sort of religious practice.

Homo sapiens today
This is the scientific name we use for modern people today. *Homo sapiens* replaced *Homo neanderthalensis* about 35,000 years ago. These early members of our species produced amazing art. Later *Homo sapiens* went on to invent farming and to develop civilizations.

LUCY
The most complete example of an *Australopithecus* female skeleton was found in Ethiopia in 1974. She was about 20 years old when she died. She was named Lucy because the anthropologists were talking about the Beatles' song "Lucy in the Sky with Diamonds" in the archaeologists' camp at the time the bones were discovered!

Where People Lived?

There are about 4 billion people living in the world today. Very few places have no people living in them, and it is difficult to imagine huge areas of the world with no human beings.

While human ancestors, *Homo ergaster*, were living in Africa, other groups, like *Homo erectus* lived in Java and China 1.5 million years ago. People were living in Europe 700,000 years ago.

Not all parts of the world could be inhabited. Some areas were very difficult to live in. Much of the surface of Europe was covered by ice as late as 10,000 years ago. While Europe was in the Ice Ages, the Sahara region of Africa was even drier than it is today, and no one could live there.

Two huge areas of the world remained uninhabited for a long time—the Americas and Australia. Forty thousand years ago, North America was joined to Asia by a land bridge. Hunters had moved across into North America 30,000 years ago. But great areas of what is now the United States and Canada were still covered by ice. Hunters could only move along narrow areas of land free from ice. Nevertheless, by 9000 B.C., people had reached the southern tip of South America.

There were hunters in Australia and New Guinea 40,000 years ago. People moved to islands such as Tonga and Samoa, but it was another 2,000 years before there were people living on Easter Island (see page 22).

Mesa Verde
From about A.D. 1000 the Anasazi people lived in houses built under the protection of a cliff. The site was discovered in 1874.

North America

Americas
30,000 years ago – first hunters cross from Asia to America
12,000 B.C. – first people in Central America
9000 B.C. – first people reach tip of South America

Mesa Verde

Atlantic Ocean

Vikings
The Vikings reached North America by about A.D. 1000

Easter Island

South America

Easter Island
People first reached Easter Island, from the Marquesas and Society Islands, around A.D. 500. Around A.D. 1000 the inhabitants started to carve huge stone statues.

Stonehenge
Probably the most famous stone circle in the world, Stonehenge was begun around 3000 B.C. Stone was hauled from as near as 18 miles (30 km) and as far as 120 miles (200 km) away from its site in southern England.

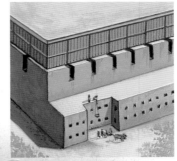

Mohenjo-Daro
The first cities in India were built near the Indus River around 2500 B.C. There were about 40,000 people living in Mohenjo-Daro. The city even had its own garbage disposal system.

Europe
700,000 years ago – first people living in Europe
120,000 years ago – Neanderthals, the first people to bury their dead
40,000 years ago – last Ice Age
30,000 years ago – first cave art

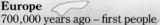
Stonehenge

Great Wall

Pyramids
Built over 3,000 years ago, these extraordinary structures were special burial monuments for ancient Egyptian kings.

Asia

Pyramids

Mohenjo-Daro

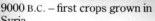

Africa
3.7 million years ago – first ape/human creatures
2 million years ago – earliest genus like us today
35,000 years ago – first *Homo sapiens*
10,000 years ago – first hunters' camps in Sahara after last Ice Age

Central Asia and Near East
9000 B.C. – first crops grown in Syria
4400 B.C. – horse domesticated on the Steppes of Central Asia
3500 B.C. – first civilizations in Sumeria

Laetoli

Great Wall of China
The first emperor of China began building a wall over 2,000 years ago as a line of defense. Completed in 1644, the wall stretches 1,500 miles (2,300 km) from the Yellow Sea to Central Asia.

Pacific Ocean

Asia, Australia, and Oceania
1.5 million years ago – *Homo erectus* in China and Java
450,000 years ago – first humans in China
40,000 years ago – people in Australia and New Guinea
6000 B.C. – first farming villages in China
4500 B.C. – farming around Ganges River, India

Australia

Laetoli
The oldest footprints in the world—3.7 million years old—were found in Tanzania in East Africa in 1976. Further discoveries in this part of the world show that our ancestors have been around a long, long time.

People Lived in Caves?

Have you ever seen cartoons about cave people? Apart from the Flintstones, they usually show "primitive" people living in caves during the Ice Ages long ago.

Some of the earliest hunters did live in caves or in cave shelters in various parts of the world. As you will see on these pages, people have lived in caves right up until modern times.

Caves provided good shelter for early peoples and protection against wild animals, especially if a fire was lit at the entrance. Even overhanging cliffs gave the hunters some kind of roof. Whole towns were built under cliffs in what is now the United States (see page 9).

The early inhabitants of caves left behind the remains of camp fires, animal bones, and tools for archaeologists to **excavate**. But perhaps the most remarkable cave finds have been the paintings of the hunters of the Ice Ages in Europe. The artists have given us extraordinary pictures of the animals that lived at the time.

Painting in caves
Artists were painting walls and ceilings of caves in Europe 30,000 years ago. The most famous painted caves are at Lascaux in France, and Altamira in Spain. The artists also carved in bone and stone, and made little figures of clay, which were probably religious idols. Most of the paintings are deep in the caves and not in the rock shelters (see below) where the hunters actually lived.

Sheltering in caves
In the Dordogne area in southwestern France, there are a number of cliff and cave shelters used by hunters. Among them is this cave shelter at Le Madeleine, which had people living in it about 12,000 years ago. The people who lived here probably divided the shelter into rooms, with partitions made from wood and animal skins. Their weapons and tools were made from flint, bone, and wood. The people of La Madeleine also built camps as they followed the herds of animals they hunted for food.

Cave refuse
Danger Cave (shown below) lies on the edge of the Great Salt Lake Desert, in Utah. It was a home to hunters from about 8300 B.C. They left behind large quantities of garbage, 12 feet (4 m) high, inside the cave!

Cave dwellers in the 19th century
The last cave dweller in Great Britain lived in the cave shown above in 1928 in the Midlands. The caves were first occupied in the 19th century and were fully equipped with windows and furniture!

Living under cliffs
The Anasazi people, who lived in the southern part of the United States, built this fantastic settlement, shown above, under a cliff at Mesa Verde, in Colorado. You can see a large number of buildings, towers, and circular rooms. These rooms were used as meeting places and for ceremonies. Mesa Verde was occupied from about A.D. 1000 to about A.D. 1300.

What Materials People Worked with Long Ago?

Look around you before you continue to read this section. Perhaps you are at home, in school, or in a library. What surrounds you—furniture, walls, a whole range of objects in the room? What are they made of? You will see things made of metal, glass, plastic, and wood.

Now think about what materials people might have used in the past. Remember there were no factories or scientific ways of converting raw materials. People certainly didn't use plastic. What did they use?

Materials that they could find naturally were the only choice—stone, wood, **fibers**, bones, and skins from animals. Stone tools that are 2.5 million years old have been found. Metal was discovered much later, as you will see below. Some raw materials, like stone and metal, had to be dug out of the ground. Not all the objects that people used in the past survived until today. Things made of material that rots (like wood and bone) are not found as often as stone and metal objects.

BONE AND WOOD

You might think that bone and wood were used by prehistoric hunters only for tools and weapons. In fact, bone was carved into all sorts of useful and decorative objects, even into modern times. In the 19th century people used combs and toothbrushes (with hair bristles) made of bone.

Wood has been used since the earliest peoples. Once people discovered how to use flint, wood could be worked and sharpened into new types of weapons.

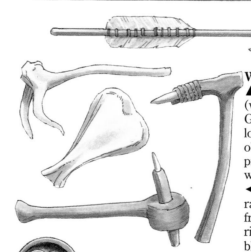

Weapons and Tools

▲ Weapons used by the Inuit people (whom we used to call Eskimos) in Greenland and North America. The longest object here is a spear. The object at the top is for catching fish. Its prongs are made from the tusks of a walrus.

◄ Tools of the prehistoric farmer. Top: rake from a deer antler. Left: shovel from a cow's shoulder blade. Bottom and right: wooden handled axes with flint blades.

Casting bronze
Chinese bronze workers from about 1600 B.C. The bronze is **cast** using the "lost wax" method. The original object is made from wax, surrounded by soft clay, and fired, making the wax run out. The hard clay mold then has bronze poured into it.

Mount for a horse harness, England, around 100 B.C.

Bronze pin made from a stone mold

Bridle piece for a horse, England, around 100 B.C.

Gold bracelet, England, around 100 B.C.

Drinking cup made of bronze, from around 100 B.C.

Two bronze weapon heads from China, from around 1500 B.C.

METALS

In about 6000 B.C. some people in central Europe discovered that copper **ore** could be mined from the ground and beaten into shapes. Later metalworkers began to melt the ore and pour it into stone molds. By about 2800 B.C., people discovered that, if you added tin to copper, you got a harder metal, called bronze. Iron, the hardest metal in prehistoric times, was discovered around 2000 B.C. in western Asia.

10

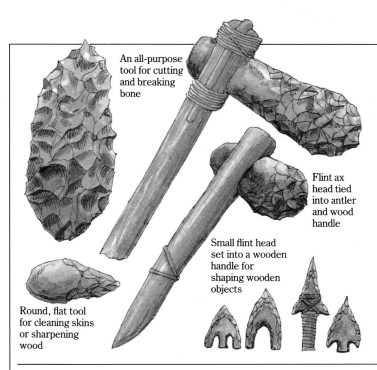

An all-purpose tool for cutting and breaking bone

Flint ax head tied into antler and wood handle

Small flint head set into a wooden handle for shaping wooden objects

Round, flat tool for cleaning skins or sharpening wood

FLINT

Flint is a stone that was used throughout the world by prehistoric peoples for all kinds of tools and weapons. The earliest tools were roughly shaped to fit into the hand and used for cutting. Later, skilled flint workers made the finest knives and **arrowheads** from blocks of flint. About 4,000 years ago, people in Europe were mining flint from pits cut deep into the ground.

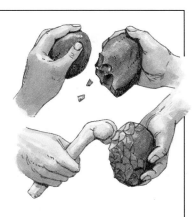

Arrowheads of flint

▼ Wooden bows
Wooden bow with a fiber string and arrows (above). Bows are rarely found, but the arrowheads made of flint (described in the section above) often survive. This weapon was used mainly for hunting but was also useful in warfare.

◄ Making fire
This is one way *Homo sapiens* used to make fire 1.5 million years ago. A little bow with a wooden drill of hard wood was set on a flat piece of wood (left). The wooden pieces rubbed together, smoldered, and ignited dried grasses.

Beaker
This pot was made in Great Britain around 2000 B.C. We call it a beaker because of its shape. The decoration was made by pressing a bone comb into the wet clay.

Greek pots
Pots made in ancient Greece were of very high quality and often showed pictures of gods or heroes.

A pot with a face made in Hungary around 4500 B.C.

CLAY
Over 10,000 years ago people began making clay into shapes and firing it to make it hard. The most useful objects made were pots for storing ingredients for meals. Pots were also used for cooking until medieval times, as pots and pans are today. Because the clay of pots has been made very hard by firing, it is difficult to destroy. Archaeologists find more pieces of pottery than anything else on most excavations.

Who Invented Writing?

People have not always written things down. The "prehistoric period" means a time before writing was invented. Prehistoric people gradually began to live in larger groups and to build towns. Their rulers collected **taxes**. Trade developed between different peoples with different languages. It was important to invent a way to keep records and pass on messages.

In the first stage in the development of writing, drawings called **pictograms** were used to describe objects. The Sumerian people, who lived between the Tigris and Euphrates rivers in present-day Iraq, were the first to draw pictograms, around 3200 B.C. The first drawings were of goods they traded or wanted a record of, such as date palms, fish, or barley.

These drawings of objects were gradually changed into picture scripts and then into symbols. The Sumerians invented a simple way of making symbols to represent the early drawings. It was called **cuneiform** writing. But other kinds of picture writing were carried on at the same time in other countries. The ancient Egyptians had a form of writing called **hieroglyphics**.

By 1000 B.C., the first alphabet was invented by the Phoenician people. This is the system used today, in which a letter stands for a sound.

HOW PAPYRUS IS MADE

Papyrus is a water plant that grows along the Nile River in Egypt. It was used by the ancient Egyptians to make an early form of paper to write on. The ancient Greeks and Romans also used papyrus to write on. The sheets of papyrus could be cleaned and then used again.

1. The papyrus plant grows along riverbanks. The Nile had the best supply of plants.

2. The stem of the plant was cut into long, thin strips with a knife.

3. Strips were laid out and more strips laid over and across them at right angles.

4. A piece of cloth held the strips down while they were flattened.

5. The papyrus was dried and polished smooth with a flat stone.

CHINESE WRITING

Examples of Chinese writing survive from about 1500 B.C. The people used pictographs at first but later developed a script. The Chinese were the first to produce books printed from woodblocks in the 9th century B.C.

EGYPTIAN HIEROGLYPHICS

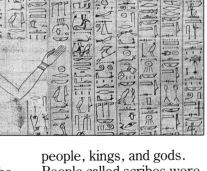

The ancient Egyptians wrote in hieroglyphs. The word means "sacred writing in stone." Many hieroglyphs were cut into stone, but others were drawn onto papyrus or painted on walls of tombs or on coffins. There was all sorts of Egyptian writing: letters, records, poems, and stories about people, kings, and gods. People called scribes were employed to draw and paint the hieroglyphic writings. Scribes would also carve into stone.

ROSETTA STONE

The Rosetta Stone, which was found in Egypt in 1799, was a vital clue in **deciphering** Egyptian hieroglyphs. The stone showed a decree made in 196 B.C. by Egyptian priests. The top section is in hieroglyphic script, the middle one in another Egyptian script, and the bottom one in ancient Greek.

CUNEIFORM WRITING

Cuneiform means "wedge-shaped writing." It was originally drawn with a sharp point onto wet clay, which could then be hardened. A combination of wedge shapes made up words. The wooden or reed "pen" was cut into a wedge shape, which could be pressed into the wet clay.

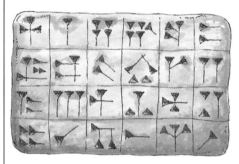

This shows how cuneiform words developed. First a simple drawing was used. Then the wedge-shaped pen marked out the shape. By the final stage, the scribes had to make sure that the symbol for each word was different.

On the left the scribe makes a separate drawing for each word. On the right the wedge-pen is used to stamp out the words.

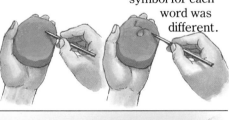

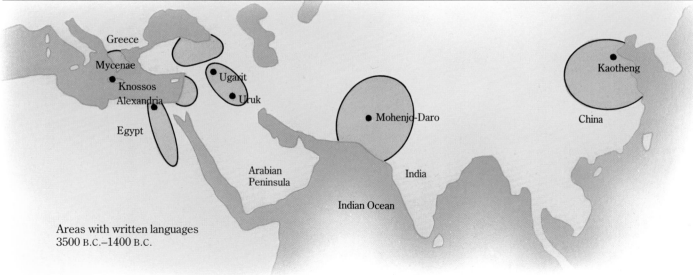

Areas with written languages
3500 B.C.–1400 B.C.

The spread of writing
The earliest writing developed in Mesopotamia around 3500 B.C. It was based on pictures, just as the Egyptian hieroglyphics that appeared 500 years later were. Evidence of later forms of writing, developed between 2500 and 1400 B.C., are found farther north in the Indus Valley and Greece. China established a written form around 1400 B.C., as did Syria and Palestine with their early alphabets.

Who Invented the Wheel?

How could we manage today without the wheel? Have you ever thought about how many different types of wheels there are all around us? There are wheels for cars and bicycles, in clocks, on CDs, and lots more. One hundred years ago, you might have thought of wheels in windmills and water wheels or the wheels on a cart.

But what did people do before wheels were invented? Archaeologists think that heavy stones (like those used to build the pyramids on page 18 and for Stonehenge on page 16, for example) might have been moved on rollers.

The first wheels were probably invented by the Sumerians (see page 24) in a country known as Mesopotamia (now modern Iraq), over 5,000 years ago. The first wheels for vehicles were solid. About 3,000 years ago the spoked wheel was invented.

Wheels were used for all kinds of things in the past. The ancient Greeks and Romans used wheels as **pulleys**, for lifting large weights, and on vehicles, for driving machinery to grind corn into flour.

THE DEVELOPMENT OF THE WHEEL

Inventors in prehistoric times must have experimented with various kinds of wheels. You can see the earliest solid wheels in the picture below from Mesopotamia. The drawing on the right shows parts of a wheel found by archaeologists in France. The wheel is nearly 3,000 years old. It doesn't have spokes, but the rim is reinforced with cross braces that fit into a central bar.

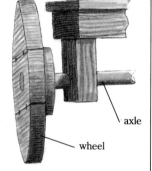

axle

wheel

Attaching wheels
The wooden pin holds the wheel onto the **axle** in the prehistoric wheel from France (left). The wheel above shows another development. Here the wheel is attached to the axle so that the axle and the wheel turn as the vehicle goes along.

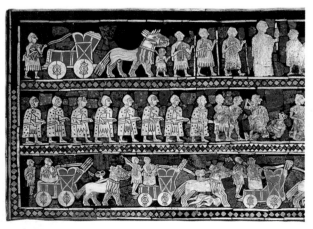

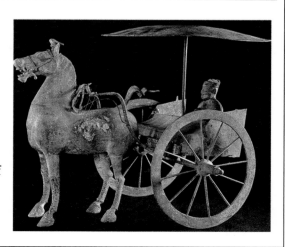

Wood or metal?
The wheels on the chariots to the left were made of wood. This decorated box, about 4,500 years old, is from Ur in Sumeria. Not all wheels were wood. Some were made of metal. This model of a Chinese chariot (right) is from the 2nd century A.D.

THE POTTER'S WHEEL

The wheel for throwing pottery was probably in use long before wheels on vehicles. The earliest prehistoric pottery was made by hand around 7000 B.C. in the Middle East. Later the Sumerians had the idea of throwing a lump of clay on a wheel. The wheel was simply spun by the potter's hand or foot.

ROMAN CART

This is a Roman long-distance coach drawn by horses. Sometimes passengers traveled on seats on the roof as well.

Journeys were always slow, bumpy, and dirty. A family might go from their town house to their country estate in a cart such as this.

Wheel technology

The development of the wheel may have occurred in the following way. The first wheels were made of a solid piece of wood cut from a tree trunk. The second stage was the invention of a wheel made from smaller planks of wood fitted together with cross pieces. Both of these early wheels were very heavy. The third stage was to try to make the wheel lighter by cutting out sections. The final stage was to make spokes. This type of wheel was much lighter but was still strong and is still used on bicycles today. Four examples of wheels are shown on the left.

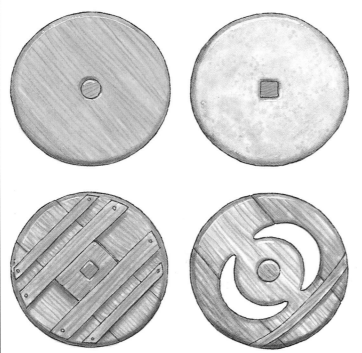

Coping with bumps

The problem with the early wooden wheels was that they usually made the vehicle move very bumpily. The invention (above) came from Denmark around 100 B.C. The rounded pegs, made of a hardwood, work like modern ball bearings by helping the rotating parts to move smoothly.

CHARIOTS

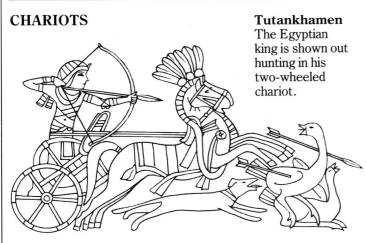

Tutankhamen
The Egyptian king is shown out hunting in his two-wheeled chariot.

A high chariot
This stone carving shows the Assyrian king Ashurbanipal riding on a high chariot in Babylon around 645 B.C. The canopy (a kind of umbrella) shows how important he was (like the Chinese official on page 14).

How Stonehenge Was Built?

The first farming people of northern Europe did not build towns, but they did put up monuments for religious ceremonies and for the burial of their dead. Circular areas were enclosed by ditches and banks of earth. Stones were set upright in the ground, sometimes on their own, sometimes in long rows, and sometimes in circles.

The most famous stone circle in the world is Stonehenge. Building began around 3000 B.C. The farming community that built it must have been rich and well organized to make such a huge construction. They probably knew how to measure accurately and had good engineers to work out how to build the monument.

Stonehenge may have been built as a temple for ceremonies and religious rituals for the farming people in that part of southern England. The circular bank and the stones were carefully measured, and the structure may have been used as a gigantic calendar to help the farming community predict the seasons of the year.

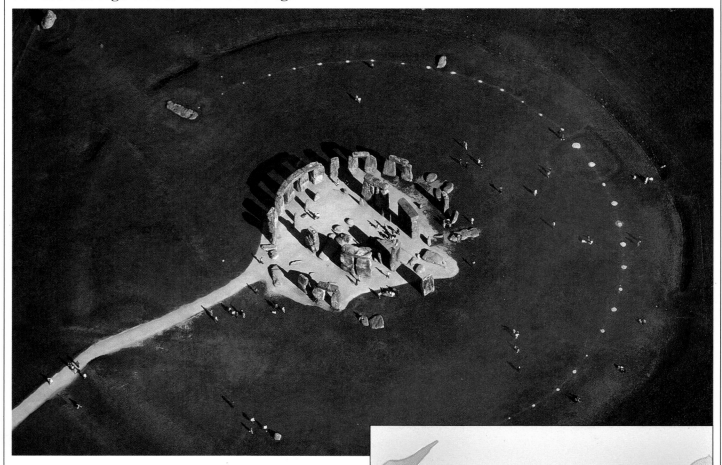

An aerial view
The best way to see how Stonehenge was built is to study it from above. You can see where the ditch marks the original circle. Look beyond the single stone in the upper lefthand corner. Two lines of ditches show where the ceremonial route approached the inner circles of stone.

Stonehenge is not a single circle of stones. It was rebuilt several times. The larger stones were brought from about 20 miles (30 km) away. The smaller ones were moved from the Prescelly Mountains in Wales, over 125 miles (200 km) away. The builders probably used rollers to move the heavy stones.

Bristol

London

Stonehenge

Southampton

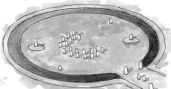

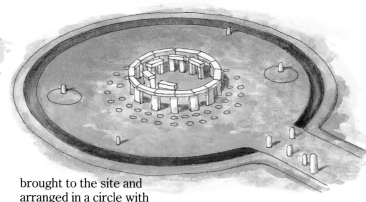

First phase

Around 3000 B.C. the people measured out and dug a circular ditch with an entrance on one side. Four stones were set up inside. The Heel Stone is placed so that the sun rises over it on the first day of summer (around June 21).

Second and third phase

Around 2100 B.C. the monument was changed. Bluestones were brought from Wales to form a double circle in the center. This construction was never finished. The biggest change came about 100 years later. Huge sandstones were brought to the site and arranged in a circle with **lintels** on top. A horseshoe arrangement was also constructed in the center.

A reconstruction

An enormous number of people must have helped in the building of Stonehenge. Each stone was roughly shaped before it was set in the ground and then pounded into its final form. The builders may have managed it using rollers, **levers**, **scaffolding**, and pulleys.

Who Built the Pyramids?

The valley of the Nile River became the birthplace of one of the world's greatest civilizations—ancient Egypt. The land was very fertile and produced more than enough food for the population. Egypt became a rich country with a ruler called a **pharaoh**. The Egyptians were good **engineers** and architects, and constructed many extraordinary buildings, including temples and palaces, which were built by a large slave population.

The most famous of the ancient Egyptian buildings are the pyramids. These were special monuments for the remains of their pharaohs. The **mummified** body of the pharaoh was carried in a coffin along with a huge number of precious objects, clothes, furniture, and statues. All this was brought by boats along the Nile, carried to the special building, and placed in different tombs within the pyramid.

The first pyramids were built in steps, but Egyptian architects then learned how to construct the smooth-sided ones shown in the photograph. From about 1550 B.C. Egyptian kings were buried in tombs cut out of the rock in the "Land of the Dead" near the city of Thebes.

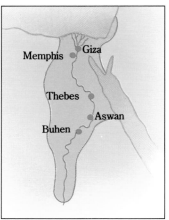

The great pyramids
Pyramids at Giza near Cairo, the modern capital of Egypt. These royal burial tombs were used from about 2700 B.C. Only part of the limestone facing of the pyramids survive, as it was stolen to build the city of Cairo. The map shows how the settlements of the ancient Egyptians are close to the Nile River.

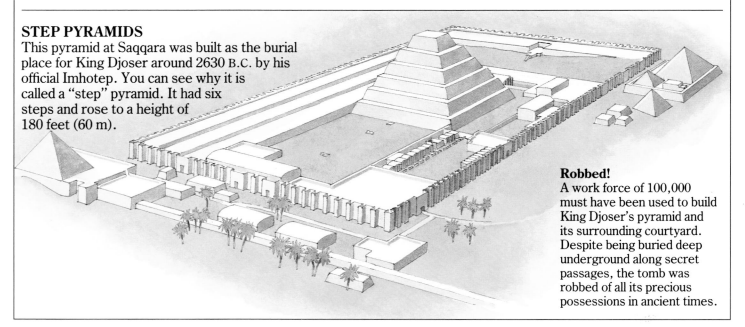

STEP PYRAMIDS
This pyramid at Saqqara was built as the burial place for King Djoser around 2630 B.C. by his official Imhotep. You can see why it is called a "step" pyramid. It had six steps and rose to a height of 180 feet (60 m).

Robbed!
A work force of 100,000 must have been used to build King Djoser's pyramid and its surrounding courtyard. Despite being buried deep underground along secret passages, the tomb was robbed of all its precious possessions in ancient times.

Huge pyramid

The Great Pyramid at Giza (photograph left) was built from about 6.5 million tons of stone. Single blocks weighed anything between 2 and 15 tons each. The stone was brought to the site by boats along the Nile. The workers lived in temporary towns on site.

BUILDING STAGES

The first stage in building a pyramid was to get the site level. A square of sand was cleared down to the solid rock below. Then trenches were dug over the site and water let in from the Nile River. Because water finds its own level, it was easy to see where the high and low spots were.

Next the builders used rectangular and triangular blocks of stone to form a perfect square, starting in the middle. Triangular blocks were used on the outside. To add the layers, builders constructed a great ramp made of earth and bricks beside them. The last block to be added was pyramid-shaped. Finally the builders removed the ramp.

Who Built the Great Wall of China?

It was the first emperor of China who was responsible for the Great Wall. His name was Emperor Ch'in Shih Huang Ti, and the country was named China after him. He united the country in 221 B.C. Before that the different cities of China had been at war for 250 years. His family, or **dynasty**, ruled China for only eleven years, but the system of government that he set up lasted until 1912.

Before the Emperor Ch'in, there were seven states in China, each with its own king. They fought wars against each other and tried to protect themselves by building defenses to the north. They built a series of earth walls to keep foreigners from invading their lands.

Ch'in Shih Huang Ti decided to construct a single line of defense across the northern edge of his kingdom. He had the earlier walls joined together and started building a stone wall with watchtowers.

But it was not only the Great Wall that was constructed while Ch'in Shih Huang Ti was emperor. He ordered a whole system of new roads and canals to be built. Under his rule, laws, money, writing, and weights and measures were made the same throughout China.

The emperor also ordered an incredible burial place to be built for himself. It was discovered in 1974, when archaeologists uncovered a gigantic tomb under the ground. It contained about 10,000 full-size clay models of warriors and servants. In earlier years some rulers in China ordered their servants and bodyguards to be buried alive with them when they died.

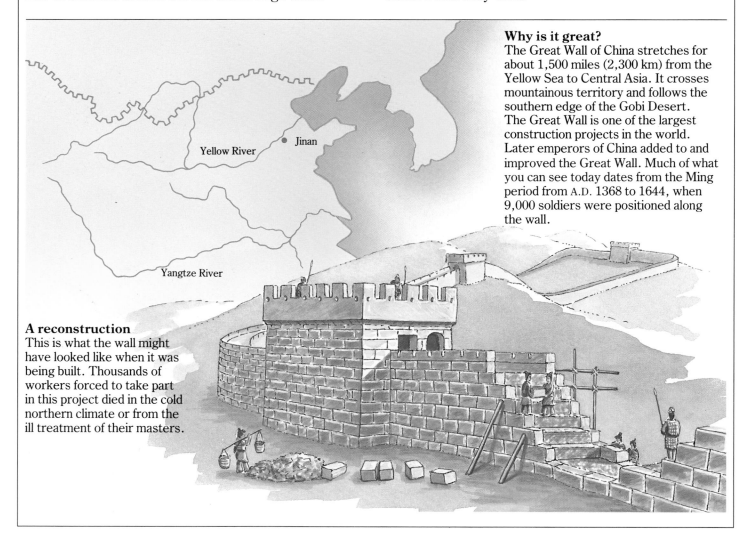

Why is it great?
The Great Wall of China stretches for about 1,500 miles (2,300 km) from the Yellow Sea to Central Asia. It crosses mountainous territory and follows the southern edge of the Gobi Desert. The Great Wall is one of the largest construction projects in the world. Later emperors of China added to and improved the Great Wall. Much of what you can see today dates from the Ming period from A.D. 1368 to 1644, when 9,000 soldiers were positioned along the wall.

Yellow River • Jinan

Yangtze River

A reconstruction
This is what the wall might have looked like when it was being built. Thousands of workers forced to take part in this project died in the cold northern climate or from the ill treatment of their masters.

A barrier

You can see what a barrier the Great Wall was to China's enemies from the north. The wall is a great bank of earth faced with stone and standing about 30 feet (9 m) high. It was defended by guard towers and gateways. Warnings of attack could be given by signal fires along the wall. Soldiers could easily travel along the wide roadway measuring 16 feet (4.5 m) wide, on top of the wall. Archers in the guard towers protected sections of the wall.

The emperor

Ch'in Shih Huang Ti, the first emperor of China, died in 210 B.C. after uniting the country under one system of government. After his death, his eldest son took over the kingdom, but his younger son soon forced the oldest son to abdicate, and the younger son became ruler instead.

Who Made the Easter Island Statues?

Easter Island is in the Pacific Ocean, 2,300 miles (3,700 km) west of Chile in South America. We know it as Easter Island because the first European to find it was Admiral Roggeveen, from Holland, who landed on Easter Day 1722. He reported that the inhabitants of the island believed that their neighbors lived on the moon. But where had these people come from?

By 1000 B.C., people traveled from Indonesia to the nearest islands of the Pacific Ocean: Samoa and Tonga. Around A.D. 300 the people from these islands were on the move again and settled in some groups of islands to the east. By A.D. 500, people from the Marquesas and Society Islands had discovered Easter Island.

Where are the islands?
The Pacific Ocean is an enormous area to cross, even today in modern ships. The early settlers of the Pacific islands traveled in dugout canoes, like the one in this drawing. These boats had to cover a vast distance. By A.D. 650, all the islands of Polynesia had been settled. New Zealand may have been inhabited for over 15,000 years.

The island was thickly wooded, and the new arrivals started to clear trees and to grow bananas, yams, and taro plants. They also kept animals, such as chickens, pigs, dogs, and rats, for food. By the time Admiral Roggeveen arrived on the island, there were only a few trees left.

The statues, which are called *moai*, are giant carvings of torsos (the upper part of the body to the waist). But the original settlers of Easter Island did not build these statues. They did make the great platforms of stone facing the sun. But it was not until about A.D. 1000 that people started to carve the huge statues.

South America

Australia

Easter Island

New Zealand

PUTTING UP THE STATUES

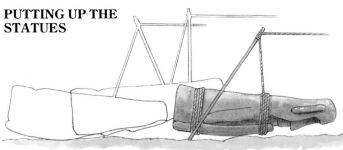

We are not sure how the people of Easter Island moved and put up the huge stone statues. We think this is how they did it:
1. The carved statue had a wooden sled tied to it.

2. A triangular-shaped trestle was used to move the statue slowly along on its sled.
3. The statue was then levered and pulled upright onto its stone platform.

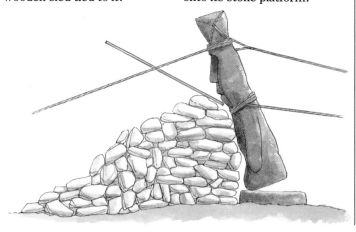

Warring islanders
In the late 18th and early 19th centuries, the great statues were all pushed over face downward by the Easter Island people, who were continually at war with each other. These statues at Ahu Akivi were restored and put up again in 1961. The statues stand on stone platforms called *ahus*.

Waiting to be finished
There are about 600 statues on Easter Island. They were carved from stone, called tufa, from the volcano Rano Raraku. Some of these statues were waiting to be finished before removal to sites elsewhere on the island. Most of the statues are 13–16 feet (4–5 m) tall, but some are 66 feet (20 m) tall and weigh about 300 tons! Once they were set up, the statues had eyes of white coral added and the body carved and painted to show bright tattoos.

Who Built the First Cities?

Today we call highly organized societies "civilizations." One of the most important things to happen in a civilization is the building of cities. In the land of Sumeria, between the Tigris and Euphrates rivers in present-day Iraq, were the world's first cities. This land is also known as Mesopotamia which, in Greek, meant "the land between the rivers." Very large numbers of people could live together in cities because the land was very **fertile**. It produced enough food to support not only the farmers but also engineers, administrators, priests, and rulers.

These early cities are often called city-states, because each city controlled territory around them. They were like small countries. Each city was ruled by a king who collected taxes from the people and built great public buildings and palaces.

The earliest civilization was in Sumeria around 3500 B.C. Civilizations with cities developed in other parts of the world as well around 2500 B.C. in the Andes in South America, 2500 B.C. in India, and 2200 B.C. in China.

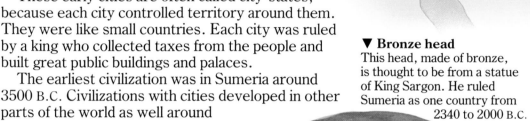

▼ Bronze head
This head, made of bronze, is thought to be from a statue of King Sargon. He ruled Sumeria as one country from 2340 to 2000 B.C.

▲ Sumeria
The land of Sumeria, or Sumer, was able to support large numbers of people from the fertile plain. The most important cities of Sumeria are shown on this map.

THE CITY OF UR

Ur was one of the most important cities in Sumeria. By about 2500 B.C., there were probably 20,000 people living inside the walled city. Ur had a long history. It started as a small settlement around 4500 B.C.

One feature of Sumerian cities was the temple-tower, called a **ziggurat**. The one shown here was completed in Ur around 2100 B.C., and it dominated the city. It was a temple to the moon god of the Sumerians, Nannar. The ziggurat stands inside a sacred walled enclosure surrounded by the houses of the people of the city.

THE INDUS VALLEY

Another important civilization developed in the Indus Valley in Pakistan. By about 3500 B.C., there were farming settlements here on the fertile land around the Indus River. By 2500 B.C., cities such as Mohenjo-Daro and Harappa, with populations of about 40,000, were being built. These cities were well organized and laid out in a regular pattern. There were even proper water and sewage systems. The city authorities also maintained a garbage disposal system. Archaeologists have also found a number of one-room buildings, which may have been for the city's police force.

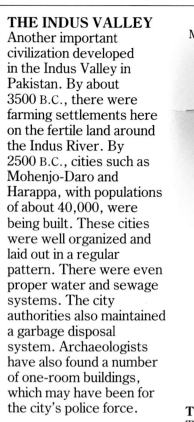

Homes and warehouses

Above is a house with an open inner courtyard, which gave light to the rooms around it. The house had its own bathroom. Below right is a huge warehouse used for storing and distributing grain.

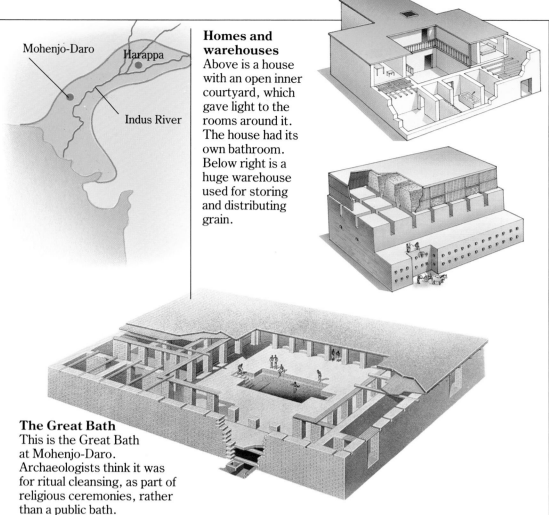

The Great Bath

This is the Great Bath at Mohenjo-Daro. Archaeologists think it was for ritual cleansing, as part of religious ceremonies, rather than a public bath.

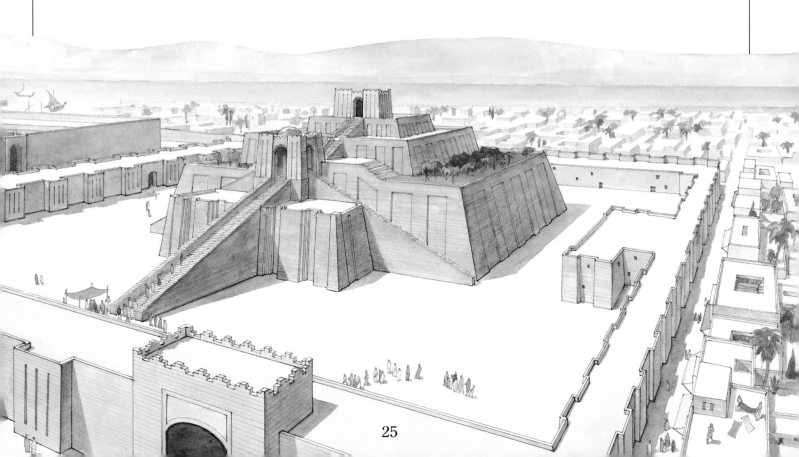

What Babylon Was Like?

Mesopotamia, "the land between the rivers," had been fought over and conquered by several peoples. One of its independent kingdoms was called Babylonia. The most famous of all the kings of Babylonia was King Nebuchadrezzar, who defeated the invading Egyptians in 605 B.C. He rebuilt the capital city, called Babylon.

The city was heavily defended by several walls. Nine impressive gateways led into the city. Everywhere you looked you could see the great public buildings of Babylon. You could also enter Babylon by boat, as the Euphrates River ran through the center of the city. A canal joined the river to the moat, which protected the city's walls.

The Babylonian Empire grew until all the land from the Persian Gulf to the Mediterannean Sea was ruled from Babylon. But in 539 B.C. the empire was attacked by the Persians, Babylon was captured, and a new civilization arrived in Mesopotamia.

The ruins of Babylon were discovered by German archaeologists in 1899. Many of the ruins were excavated. The Iraqi government has begun to restore many of the structures.

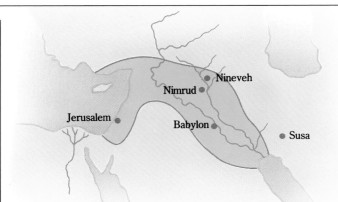

The Babylonian Empire
The Euphrates River runs through the city of Babylon. Under Nebuchadrezzar, the Babylonian Empire grew until it reached the Mediterranean Sea.

The city of Babylon
Babylon (below) must have been a splendid place in Nebuchadrezzar's time. This was the great ziggurat (see page 24) and the Temple of Marduk, the god of the city. The Euphrates River is in the foreground. In the background you can see the houses of the ordinary people of the city.

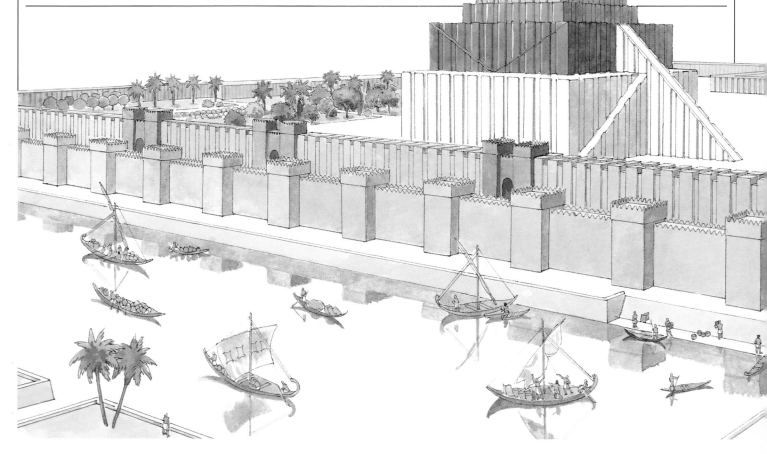

THE HANGING GARDENS

One of the Seven Wonders of the Ancient World was the Hanging Gardens of Babylon—an **oasis** in a hot dusty city. This is what they may have been like based on descriptions by ancient writers. These beautiful terraced gardens were said to have been built by King Nebuchadrezzar for his wife, Amitiya. She was the daughter of the king of the Medes, who lived in mountainous lands to the north. The gardens were said to remind Amitiya of her green homeland.

Gates into the city

This is a reconstruction of one of the gateways into Babylon—the Marduk Gate. The god of the city, Marduk, was represented as a dragon. There are dragons all over the gate. The gate was built of bricks held together by **bitumen**. All over the outside are tiles, including those that make up each dragon. (Below) One of the gates of the city stood between the Euphrates River and the eastern half of the city.

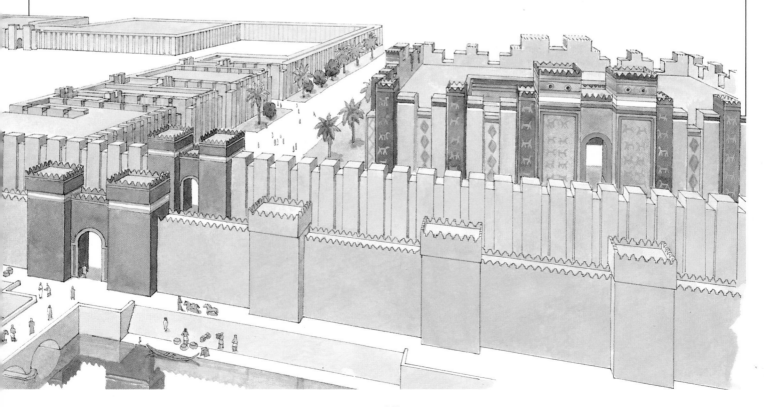

What People Ate in the Past?

Around 12,000 years ago, in the lands between the Red Sea and the Persian Gulf, the climate began to change. The Ice Ages were coming to an end, and the weather became wetter. Trees and wild grasses began to grow. The hunters who lived there began to farm the land by taming animals and collecting the wild grasses. The first farm animals were goats. Then around 11,000 years ago, sheep were kept, and wheat was grown in Mesopotamia. We know that around 9,000 years ago people were keeping pigs in Turkey, and the remains of cattle from around 8,000 years ago have been found in northern Africa and around the Aegean Sea. Meanwhile, in Peru in South America, wild grasses and beans were being cultivated about 10,500 years ago.

In different parts of the world, people in the past cooked a great variety of food in all kinds of ways. Some of the recipes are still used today, but others seem strange to us. For example, the ancient Mexicans ate grasshoppers, and the Aztecs ate worms!

Great changes in eating were brought about by world travel. The Spanish introduced chickens, cows, various vegetables, wheat, bananas, rice, and sugarcane to the people of the Americas. The Americas sent such foods as potatoes, red and green peppers, peanuts, a variety of beans, pineapples, and the turkey to Europe.

Marco Polo, who traveled from Italy to China in the 13th century, reported that the Mongol armies of Russia drank the blood of their horses and prepared dried milk to take with them on journeys. Many centuries earlier, a route called the Silk Road went from China to the Mediterranean Sea. As early as 550 B.C., Chinese silk was being imported into Greece. Cinnamon and rhubarb also came from China, while coconuts and spices (pepper was the most important) came from India.

EGYPTIAN FOOD AND DRINK

Ancient Egyptian food was very healthy. People grew plenty of vegetables in the fertile fields along the Nile River. The river was full of fresh fish. People hunted game, trapped wild birds, and bred animals on farms. A typical meal for the rich would consist of bread, soup, and a fish or meat dish, followed by fresh fruit. For the poor it was likely to be bread and onions. Everyone ate with their fingers. The ancient Egyptians also pickled little birds and exported fish caught in the Nile River.

Little variety

There wasn't an enormous variety of food available for the ancient Egyptians (above). The painting from an Egyptian tomb (far left) shows an important source of food. Geese are being counted and put into baskets for the market by tradesmen.

The national drink in Egypt was beer made from barley mashed together with water. There was wine as well, but it was only available to rich Egyptians. Wine or beer might be served from a painted jug (left).

LINDOW MAN'S LAST MEAL

You can see a photograph of the remains of Lindow Man on page 38. He was an extraordinary specimen from Celtic Britain. He was so well preserved that archaeologists have been able to study the contents of his stomach. We actually know what he ate before he was sacrificed to the gods in a peat bog! In his stomach were the remains of two kinds of wheat (called emmer and spelt) and barley. Along with these grains were some wild plants—Fat Hen, Dock, and Cow Parsley.

The food had all been finely ground up into flour. It was probably made into a sort of whole wheat bread and baked over a heather and moss fire, as there were traces of them both in his stomach.

Recipe for Celtic whole wheat bread

You will need: 4 ounces (100 g) of stone-ground whole wheat flour. Mix with some barley flour. Add 5 tablespoons of water and stir into a stiff paste. Form into small, flat cakes and cook under a very hot grill for 2–3 minutes on each side. OR fry the cakes in a little fat in a frying pan. OR wrap them around a sharp stick and cook on an open fire.

EGYPTIAN AND ROMAN CANDY

Here are some recipes for ancient Egyptian and ancient Roman candy.

Egyptian: Blend 8 ounces (200 g) of dates with a little water. Add a little cinnamon, cardamom, and chopped walnuts. Shape into balls and coat in honey and ground almonds.

Roman: Take the stones out of the dates and stuff either with nuts or kernels of ground pepper. Roll in salt and fry in warmed honey.

ROMAN COOKING

The Romans were able to buy all kinds of food—fresh, salted, and pickled—in their markets. Some of their food seems very strange to us today. They ate flamingos and ostrich! A great delicacy for a rich Roman family were dormice. They were fattened on nuts in specially made clay pots with air holes in them. The dormice were stuffed with minced pork and various flavorings before being roasted in an oven. The Romans liked a lot of different flavors in their food, not just spices but specially made sauces. A favorite dish was called *liquamen*, made from salted fish and fish insides.

Roman recipe

To make cabbages with leeks, put the boiled cabbages into a shallow pot and season with *liquamen*, oil, wine, and the spice, cumin. Sprinkle with pepper, chopped leeks, caraway seeds, and fresh coriander.

Utensils

Roman cooks used a lot of pots made from fired clay for storage, mixing, and for cooking on the fire. The one on the far right is called a mortar. It's a clay mixing bowl for grinding up ingredients. It has little pieces of grit added to the inside surface to help the process. The Romans did not use forks, but they did have knives and various sizes of spoons. There was even a recipe book, which we can still read today. It was published in the 1st century A.D. by Marcus Apicius.

How People Traveled?

Today many people make long journeys in airplanes, trains, cars, or buses. In the past, especially in prehistoric times, people could not travel as easily, although sometimes it was necessary, because whole nations or tribes had to move to find new lands, just as **refugees** do in our modern world.

There were few means of transportation. At first, of course, people went on foot. Hunters followed herds of animals. Then, around 6,000 years ago, the horse was tamed in southern Russia. At first it was bred to be eaten, but it was later used for riding and to pull carts. The horse became very important to people in Asia and Europe.

Trails were important for hunting peoples and for the early farmers. But people of the great civilizations throughout the world, including China, Mesopotamia, South America, and Europe, built good roads.

Many early peoples explored new lands by sea. Some, like the Vikings, traveled thousands of miles. But the people who traveled the farthest were the peoples of Polynesia (see opposite) who sailed all over the Pacific Ocean.

THE HORSE

An ancient horse
Prehistoric peoples in southern Russia and Asia tamed the wild horse. The only true wild horse surviving today is the Przewalski's horse, shown above, a wild horse from Mongolia, living in the cold desert.

Skilled horsemen
The Scythians were **nomadic** peoples from Asia and Russia. They were skilled horse riders. Here is one Scythian warrior (right), shown on an ornament made in the 4th century B.C., riding a horse using stirrups attached to a saddle.

The Greeks learned the art of riding horses from the Scythians. This mosaic picture (below) shows one of the battles of Alexander the Great, who is on horseback on the left. Alexander became king of Macedonia, in northern Greece, in 336 B.C. He went on to conquer a huge empire, which stretched as far as India. Here Alexander is defeating the king of Persia, Darius.

ON THE SEA

The first boats used by prehistoric hunters were canoes made out of trees or animal skins stretched over wooden frames. Recently archaeologists have found a wooden ship that was probably used to carry people across the English Channel nearly 3,500 years ago. Some large ships were rowed, such as Greek and Roman warships and Viking longships. We know that the Sumerians also had boats. Below is a picture from a seal or sign used to mark someone's property. This boat is being moved with a pole.

▲ Records on vases

The ancient Greeks liked to decorate their vases, plates, and jugs with pictures. This picture is taken from the story of the hero, Odysseus, returning from the war against the Trojans. Here he has ordered his men to tie him to the ship's mast so that he would not give in to the voices of the Sirens, partly human creatures who would have lured him away and killed him.

▼ Polynesian ship

The people of the Pacific (see Easter Island page 22) sailed in boats like the one below. Their journeys were often up to 1,800 miles (3,000 km) long. Their boats were dugout canoes joined together. Of the early peoples, Polynesians sailed the farthest.

► Bayeux Tapestry

Norman ships landed on the south coast of England. The story of the invasion of England by William of Normandy, in A.D. 1066, is told on the Bayeux Tapestry, a needlework picture William had embroidered after his victory.

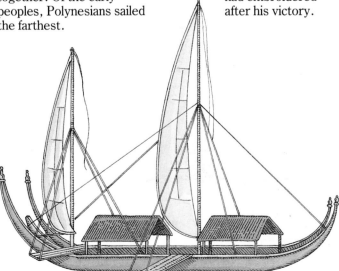

Nomadic life

Some Native Americans used a travois for carrying supplies, equipment, and children. It consisted of two poles tied together at the front and spread wide at the back. Before the Europeans introduced horses to the Native Americans, dogs were used to haul the travois. Native Americans covered about 5 miles (8 km) a day as they followed the herds to new hunting grounds.

Who Reached the Americas First?

If you look at a map of the Americas, you will see that it is a huge landmass surrounded by oceans. But 40,000 years ago, the area we now know as Alaska was joined to Asia by a land bridge. We think that it was around this time that huge herds of mammoths, mastodons, bison, reindeer, and horses crossed the land bridge. Hunters of northern Asia followed the herds. They were the first people to reach the Americas.

The small bands of hunters, like these people below, had to be on the move to kill animals for food. They used flint and other stone to make their tools and weapons, such as axes and spears. Their houses were tents made from wooden poles and covered with animal skins.

As the herds moved south, so did the hunters. By about 8000 B.C., people in South America were beginning to farm their land. By the time the first explorers sailed across the Atlantic Ocean from Europe, there were already huge civilizations in the Americas.

CHRISTOPHER COLUMBUS

Christopher Columbus was an Italian sea captain who persuaded the Spanish rulers Ferdinand and Isabella to pay for an expedition to discover a sea route to the east. In 1492 Columbus set sail with three ships and reached an island in what is now called the Bahamas. He called it San Salvador, but thought that he had sailed to islands off the coast of the East Indies! Because of this, he called the people that he found there "Indians."

Columbus sailed back to Spain to report his discovery and made three more voyages across the Atlantic Ocean. He still believed he had reached the Eastern countries when he died in 1506.

All the islands in the Caribbean Sea came under the control of Spain. The Spanish moved into Mexico and Peru. They conquered and destroyed the Aztec and the Inca empires.

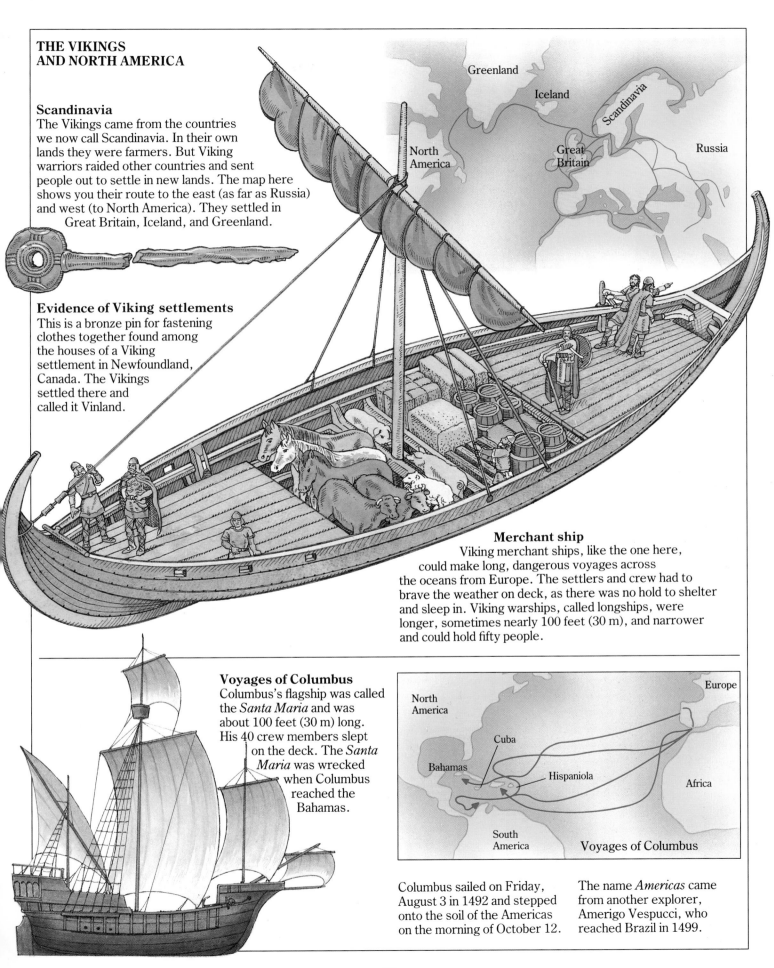

THE VIKINGS AND NORTH AMERICA

Scandinavia

The Vikings came from the countries we now call Scandinavia. In their own lands they were farmers. But Viking warriors raided other countries and sent people out to settle in new lands. The map here shows you their route to the east (as far as Russia) and west (to North America). They settled in Great Britain, Iceland, and Greenland.

Evidence of Viking settlements

This is a bronze pin for fastening clothes together found among the houses of a Viking settlement in Newfoundland, Canada. The Vikings settled there and called it Vinland.

Merchant ship

Viking merchant ships, like the one here, could make long, dangerous voyages across the oceans from Europe. The settlers and crew had to brave the weather on deck, as there was no hold to shelter and sleep in. Viking warships, called longships, were longer, sometimes nearly 100 feet (30 m), and narrower and could hold fifty people.

Voyages of Columbus

Columbus's flagship was called the *Santa Maria* and was about 100 feet (30 m) long. His 40 crew members slept on the deck. The *Santa Maria* was wrecked when Columbus reached the Bahamas.

Voyages of Columbus

Columbus sailed on Friday, August 3 in 1492 and stepped onto the soil of the Americas on the morning of October 12.

The name *Americas* came from another explorer, Amerigo Vespucci, who reached Brazil in 1499.

33

About the Past?

The experts who find out about the past are called archaeologists. They work like detectives, always looking for evidence and carefully recording everything they find. But what sort of evidence?

Archaeologists are on the lookout for clues to the way people lived in the past. Some study the remains of people millions of years ago; others study structures and industries of quite recent times.

Most people think that all the evidence archaeologists find has to be dug up. Some archaeologists do excavate sites that are under the ground, but others collect evidence aboveground or even below the ocean. Some study old buildings, others try to figure out what whole landscapes were like in the past. Some archaeologists work in laboratories analyzing the evidence using special techniques and equipment.

An important part of archaeologists' work is to put together all the evidence and tell the story of what they think happened in the past. You have been reading about this evidence in this book. You might see some actual remains in a museum or preserved at a site that is open to visitors.

Looking for the past

Archaeologists use all kinds of modern techniques to discover the remains of the past. Taking photographs from the air is very important. On the right you can see the outline of a Roman villa built in the southeast of Great Britain nearly 2,000 years ago. It's a large farmhouse built with three wings. The photograph is so clear that you can see the individual rooms and the corridors.

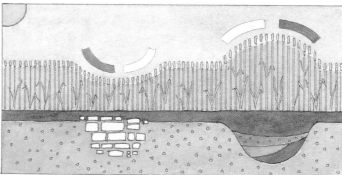

Spotting evidence

The Roman villa was discovered because the wheat crop growing in the field above the remains was stunted by the stone walls below. If there is a filled-in ditch below the surface, the crop will grow better. The sun shining at a low angle makes shadow marks, which can often be seen from an airplane.

Surface Surveying

Another way of finding evidence is through a surface survey. Sites like the Roman villa have left evidence on the surface of a field when it's been plowed. Archaeologists walking over the field will find things such as bits of building materials, broken pottery, and animal bones. The field is measured out in squares, so that all the objects can be recorded onto a map.

Uncovering the past

In places where objects from the past are in danger from modern development, archaeologists try to recover the evidence. You will often see archaeologists at work on an excavation, usually called a dig. The work must be carried out very carefully.

As they excavate using little tools, such as trowels, the archaeologists look for the remains of buildings, or perhaps areas where people have been buried in the past (see page 38–39).

The record they make must be very accurate. They take notes, make drawings and maps, take photographs, and collect figures for computer analysis.

There are usually plenty of objects found on an excavation. All these have to be carefully recorded, too. They are all marked with a code that tells the archaeologists exactly where they came from.

Archaeology in the laboratory

Archaeologists working in a laboratory have two jobs to do. They have to preserve delicate objects, and they have to find out more about them. Looking carefully at an object under a microscope might tell you more about how it was made, what it was made of, and how it was used.

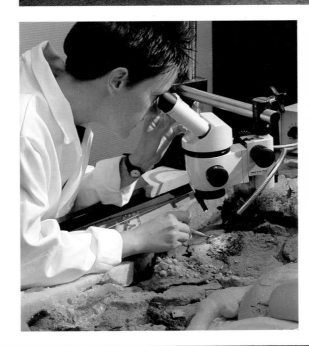

Rich evidence
This is a brooch found with the skeleton of the woman on page 39. She was buried in northern Britain in Anglo-Saxon times, around A.D. 600. On the back of the brooch, the remains of the woollen cloak she was wearing can be seen.

How Old Things Are?

How would you find out how old someone is? You might guess and say that she looked about the same age as your mother. You might ask her how old she is. You might look at her birth certificate, which would give you an accurate date. But suppose she was an Egyptian queen preserved as a mummy inside a pyramid. What would you do then?

Archaeologists have various ways of finding out the age of an object, person, or building. The age of the mummy might have been recorded on her coffin as part of an inscription. Anthropologists who study the bones of a person can help figure out the person's age.

Sometimes archaeologists can only say that an object is older or younger than other objects found near it. Archaeologists excavating a site will usually find that the farther down they dig, the older the layers and the objects in the layers are.

A number of scientific techniques discovered in this century can give dates for objects from the past. As more techniques are developed, it becomes easier for archaeologists to understand when things happened in the past.

Today in many countries of the world, we use the letters B.C. and A.D. to give dates for the past. In this system, B.C. stands for "Before Christ." All dates with B.C. after them indicate how many years backward from the date of Jesus's birth the event occurred. The letters A.D. stand for *anno Domini*, which is Latin for "in the year of our Lord." Events occurring after the birth of Jesus are shown with the letters *A.D.* followed by the year. Other peoples count their dates in different ways. The ancient Maya people of South America had a starting point for their civilization that was equal to our 3114 B.C.

FIGURING OUT A DATE

Archaeologists have not always been able to give a date for something that they have found. One of the ways in which archaeologists in the last century worked out the age of things from the past was to compare the kinds of materials used to make things. Findings show that the early people first used stone tools. Then the early people discovered metal, which was a better material to use. Archaeologists proved stone was used before metal by finding stone tools in excavations lower (therefore older) than metal ones.

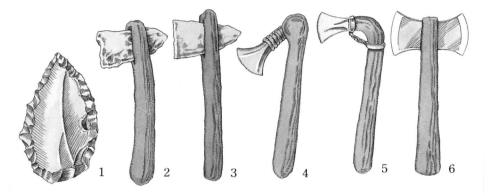

The development of the ax
The first axes (1) were held in the hand. Polished stone axes (2) were used by the earliest farmers to clear the land. The first bronze axes (3) copied stone ones. Bronze axes were developed to fit into wooden handles (4). A new development was to make a loop part of the ax (5) so that the ax head could be attached to the handle. A strong modern ax (6) has a steel head.

1. A carriage in about 1870

2. A "horseless" carriage from the 1890s

3. The first mass-produced car, the Model T Ford of 1915

4. The Lagonda car of 1947

5. A modern car

Modern sequence
Automobiles offer a good example of a modern sequence of objects that shows how design and technology develop over time. The forerunner of the modern car was the 19th century carriage (1). The first engine-driven cars looked a bit like horse-drawn carriages (2). At the beginning of this century, the car still looked a lot like a carriage (3). By about 1950, the car had changed (4). Today the car still looks something like the earlier types, but is usually much sleeker (5).

SCIENTIFIC DATING

Tree-ring dating

A system of dating lumber from ancient buildings was discovered in the United States in 1930. It is based on the fact that trees produce a new ring of growth each year. When you cut a tree down, you can simply count the rings to find out how old it is. The rings vary in their width. They are usually wider after good growing conditions and narrower after bad conditions.

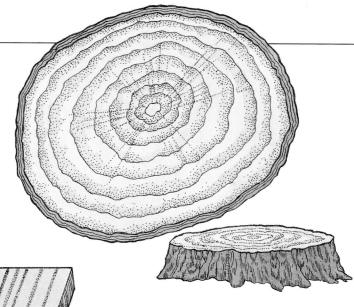

Counting growth rings

Archaeologists have identified the age of trees from the distant past. In California trees have been found that date back to 6700 B.C. Using this information, lumber from houses from the prehistoric period can be given actual dates. In Ireland trees have been dated back to 5300 B.C., and in Germany to 7500 B.C.

A fifty-year-old tree is cut down in 1992. The growth rings show a sequence.

This older tree shows some of the previous sequence of rings.

The growth rings from these two trees from the last century overlap and show that the oldest tree dates back to 1750.

Radioactive dating

It was in the 1940s that a revolution happened in archaeology. An American chemist named Willard Libby discovered a new method for dating objects from the distant past. The method is called **radiocarbon**, or carbon-14, **dating**. It works on the principle that all living things contain a certain amount of radioactive carbon. The radioactive carbon begins to decay from the moment of death. Scientists know that half of the carbon decays in 5,730 years. Measuring how much radioactive carbon is present in a specimen gives a date. This dating method can be used for remains that are 70,000 years old. Radioactivity is also used in other forms of dating, such as for measuring the dates of rocks, pottery, and glass.

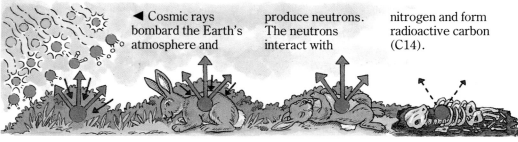

◀ Cosmic rays bombard the Earth's atmosphere and produce neutrons. The neutrons interact with nitrogen and form radioactive carbon (C14).

▲ Plants take in this radioactivity through carbon dioxide. Animals and humans take it in when they eat plants.

▲ In living plants and animals, the amount of C14 is constant. Dead plants and animals don't take in C14. Radioactivity gradually decreases.

▲ It takes 5,730 years for half the radioactive carbon to decay.

▲ The remaining radioactive carbon can be accurately measured in wood and other plant remains and in animal and human bone.

Coins

Most coins used today have the date stamped on them. Some ancient coins also have a date on them in code. This is a coin of the emperor Claudius's time. The Latin words (abbreviated) read TIberius CLAUDius CAESAR AUGustus (Emperor) Pontifex Maximus (Chief Priest) TRibunicia Potestate IIII (Chief Minister for the 4th time). Because dates of official posts were always recorded in Rome, we know this meant the year A.D. 44–45.

What People in the Past Looked Like?

How can we find out what people in the past actually looked like? You can find out what your grandparents looked like by looking at old photographs. But what about their grandparents who may have lived before photography was invented?

Sometimes we have pictures of ancient peoples from paintings or from carvings on stone. For example, we know what some ancient Romans, Greeks, Egyptians, Chinese, and Maya of Central America looked like from paintings and sculptures.

In some rare cases the actual bodies of people have been so well preserved that we do not have to use our imaginations. Bodies have survived in very wet conditions (in marshy places) or in very dry conditions (in the deserts of Egypt or the Americas). Archaeologists are sometimes able to reconstruct the appearance of someone from the past by putting together all the evidence they have collected.

RARE REMAINS

We know that the Celts (from about 700 B.C.) made sacrifices to their gods by throwing offerings into water or marshy places. Sacrifices might be fine metal objects or even live people.

In 1984 a machine cutting out wet peat from Lindow Moss near Manchester, in England, made a gruesome but fascinating find. The well-preserved remains were part of a man's body. You could even see his beard and mustache. Radiocarbon dating (see page 37) showed that the body was 2,000 years old.

The actual remains of Lindow Man

Lindow Man, as he became known, was found naked, except for a fox-fur band on his left arm. Investigations showed that he had been knocked unconscious and then strangled with a cord, which was still around his neck. His throat had been cut before he was thrown into the peat bog, probably as part of a Celtic ritual.

Tollund Man

The preserved head of a man was found in Tollund Fen, in Denmark. He was Celtic and had been hanged with a leather rope before being thrown into the water as a sacrificial victim. Tollund Man was so well preserved that archaeologists even found out that his last meal was a kind of cereal!

Lindow Man's reconstructed head

AN EGYPTIAN MUMMY

We know a lot about the appearance of ancient Egyptians because they preserved bodies through a process called mummification. The earliest Egyptian burials were in the dry, hot sands of the desert. Then a technique for preserving the body was developed. First, the internal organs were removed to stop decay inside the body. Then the body was packed in a chemical called natron for about 40 days. This dried the body out. Then the body was washed, anointed with perfumed oils, and carefully wrapped in linen bandages. The body was put in a decorated coffin.

Seneb and family

The statue to the right shows a family group from ancient Egypt. This is a man called Seneb, with his wife and children. He was chief valet and royal tutor to a pharoah. This statue was one of the earthly possessions buried with a mummy.

SKELETONS

Archaeologists often have to excavate the skeletons of people buried long ago. Studying the bones and the objects buried with the body helps build up a picture of what people were like in the past. Look at the objects with the skeleton on the right. The drawing at the bottom of the page shows what the people might have looked like. Careful study will tell what age people were, whether they suffered from diseases, and even the kinds of foods they ate.

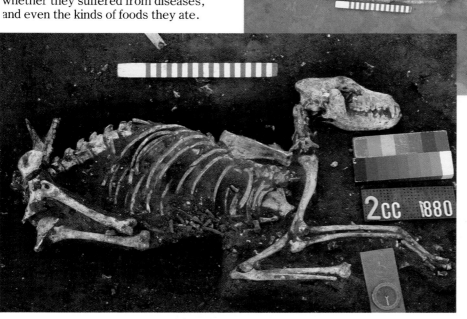

Anglo-Saxon skeletons

The two skeletons pictured above came from the cemetery of the Anglo-Saxon village of West Heslerton, in North Yorkshire. The one above is a woman buried in full dress. The one below is a hunting dog.

Reconstructions

From the careful excavation of lots of skeletons, archaeologists have been able to put together a picture of what Anglo-Saxon people were wearing about 1,500 years ago and what one of their dogs looked like!

Glossary

Archaeologists
People who study the material remains of past human life

Arrowheads
Wedged-shaped tips attached to arrows

Axle
Part of a vehicle that has the wheels connected to it

Beaker
A large cup for drinking

Bitumen
Natural substance used by ancient peoples to cement objects, such as flint arrows and spearheads to the wooden shafts

Cast
Made by pouring molten metal into two shaped pieces tied together

Cuneiform
A form of writing, invented by the Sumerians, in which wedge shapes were pushed into clay

Decipher
To work out the meaning of a language

Dynasty
A family of a king or emperor that rules a country or countries. Power is handed down from one generation to another.

Engineers
Skilled people who design and build complicated machinery or structures

Evolution
The way in which people (and other living things) develop and change over time

Excavate
To uncover or dig up remains from the past

Fertile
Used to describe land that can produce crops, such as the area around the Nile River in Egypt

Fibers
Threads that make up a piece of material for clothing

Flint
A hard rock used by prehistoric peoples to make tools and weapons

Hieroglyphics
A form of writing, used in ancient Egypt, in which drawings indicate words or letters

Levers
Bars that help lift heavy loads by using force at one point of its length

Lintels
Pieces of stone or wood that form the top part of an arch or doorway

Mummification
The process of drying and preserving a human or an animal body, used by the ancient Egyptians and others

Nomadic
Used to describe people who do not settle but choose to move around to hunt or to herd animals

Oasis
Small area in a desert region that has water and plants

Ore
Natural supply of raw metal, such as copper or iron

Organism
Living material whose separate parts work together

Papyrus
A water plant, which was used by the ancient Egyptians to make a kind of paper

Pharaoh
An ancient Egyptian ruler

Pictograms
The earliest form of writing using pictures

Pulleys
Wheels with grooves for rope that help lift heavy loads

Radiocarbon dating
A way of finding the age of an old material by measuring the amount of radioactive carbon it contains

Refugees
People who have been forced to leave their own lands and live in another country

Scaffolding
Platforms used to work above the floor or ground

Taxes
Money or goods collected by a king or government

Travois
A simple vehicle made of two trailing poles and a platform, used for carrying a load

Tree-ring dating
A way of finding the age of a wooden object by examining the growth rings and comparing them to those of a tree of known age

Ziggurats
Ancient temple-towers found in Mesopotamia

Index

© Simon & Schuster Young Books, 1993